Healthy & Whole
60 Days to Complete Wellness

Leah Lesesne, MA

Scripture quotations are from the versions below as denoted by their initials:

New American Standard Bible (NASB)
Copyright © 1960, 1962, 1963, 1968, 1971, 1972, 1973, 1975, 1977, 1995 by The Lockman Foundation

New International Version (NIV)
Holy Bible, New International Version®, NIV® Copyright ©1973, 1978, 1984, 2011 by Biblica, Inc.® Used by permission. All rights reserved worldwide.

Holman Christian Standard Bible (HCSB)
Copyright © 1999, 2000, 2002, 2003, 2009 by Holman Bible Publishers, Nashville Tennessee. All rights reserved.

English Standard Version (ESV)
The Holy Bible, English Standard Version Copyright © 2001 by Crossway Bibles, a publishing ministry of Good News Publishers.

Tree of Life Version (TLV)
Tree of Life (TLV) Translation of the Bible. Copyright © 2015 by The Messianic Jewish Family Bible Society.

Cover art icons made by www.freepik.com
from www.flaticon.com licensed by CC 3.0

ISBN: **1537100637**
ISBN-13: **978-1537100630**

Healthy & Whole

60 Days to Complete Wellness

DEDICATION

To my husband Tommy who has supported me and grown with
me on my journey to wholeness: Thank you for giving me freedom
to be my true-self and for going along with whatever new weird
wellness thing I'm into.

To Meridee, Katie, and Stef who are the best kindred spirits a girl
could ask for: Thank you for being my sounding boards and
encouragers and for insisting I write down my ideas.

ACKNOWLEDGEMENTS

Editor: Meridee Watts
Editor: Stefani McDade
App Engineer: Kyle Robinson

DISCLAIMER

I am not a doctor, licensed dietitian or licensed counselor. The information in this book should not be seen as medical, nutritional, or mental health advice and is not intended to take the place of consulting licensed health care professionals. Check with your doctor, dietitian, counselor, and/or other health professional before implementing any of the suggestions outlined in this book.

Testimony

"On the very first day of the 60 day challenge I learned that I had miscarried my first pregnancy. I was understandably heartbroken and having a really hard time with it but made a decision that the next 60 days were going to be my reset. My goals changed from health and fitness goals to mental and spiritual health goals to grieve well and be prepared to try for another pregnancy by the end of the challenge. The first 30 days the only things I had energy for was reading my Bible, doing my devotional, and keeping a journal. I didn't have much of an appetite and I rarely got to the grocery store (my poor husband) so my diet actually got worse the first month rather than better.

The second month the clouds started to clear. I was still pretty moody but I was cooking again, going to the grocery store, getting out of the house, getting my steps in, etc…. Now, at the end of the challenge, I am finally myself again and am two weeks into a workout schedule that goes beyond getting my steps in for the day. I've lost about 10 pounds (though I wasn't trying) and I feel stronger than I have in years, not just physically, but mentally and emotionally.

I think the advice I would give to those contemplating taking this challenge would be that life is going to happen over that 9 weeks, don't let that stop you from pressing in. Your goals may have to change or be tweaked but if you press into the process you will see positive change. Your health is your responsibility whether life is going well or falling apart, don't give up!"

Mary-Anne Edison

Contents

Introduction

How many times have you tried a diet to lose some weight and ended up weighing more than when you started? How many times have you tried to have a devotion and prayer time and failed to be consistent after a few days? How many times have you tried to break free from worry and anxiety only to end up worried and anxious about being worried and anxious?

These patterns of unwellness are not the fullness of life God intended for us this side of heaven. And if you've been told that this is as good as it gets – I've got good news for you. You don't have to wait until Jesus comes back to experience the Kingdom life and wellness that is available to us here and now.

"May the God of shalom make you completely whole – may your entire body-mind-spirit, be kept healthy until the coming of our Lord Jesus the Messiah."
1 Thessalonians 5:23 (author's version)

Our goal should not just be to survive. God wants us to *thrive*! He wants us to be completely whole – body-mind-spirit. And while the next 60 days may not heal you of all your diseases (Psalm 103:3), it will put you on the path towards continued growth in complete wellness.

God cares about our whole being, not just our spirits. Remember throughout this challenge that even the physical can be spiritual when we invite God into every part of our lives. "So, whether you eat or drink, or whatever you do, do all for the glory of God." 1 Corinthians 10:31 (ESV)

At times during the next 60 days, you may feel overwhelmed by the challenge, but I urge you to focus on what you *can* accomplish, not what feels out of reach. You are a triune being and your body-mind-spirit are interconnected. That is why it's important these next 60 days to not just focus on diet or devotions, but on wellness in all areas. As you work on each part simultaneously, the synergistic effect will benefit health and wholeness in every area.

Before you choose a start date for the 60 days, look over the supply list and decide which items you should purchase in advance – if not all of them. Next, take a look ahead at the weekly guides, which will instruct you on what to do for each week. Finally, familiarize yourself with the log in the back of the book – where you will track your progress going forward. Go ahead and bookmark both the *log* (starting on page 69) and the *Appendix* (starting on page 37) sections now, as you will refer to these often in the next 60 days.

The reason this challenge is 60 days instead of 30, like many other health challenges, is that it actually takes that long to form new lifestyle habits. It may take only 30 days to get into a routine, but it takes *at least* 60 days for your brain to form new pathways to support that routine – and for these behaviors to become automatic.[1]

This challenge is best completed with accountability, so try to find at least one friend to do it with you. There is also an ongoing Facebook group designed to support and encourage everyone participating in the challenge. You can join at: www.facebook.com/groups/healthywhole/

Supply List

This list is meant to be more of a guideline than a strict rulebook. The number in parenthesis at the end of each item denotes the week you will begin using it. While you will need every item, they do not need to be any particular brand or version. And if you already own some of these, you are one step closer to being ready for the challenge! For helpful links to examples and recommended items on Amazon check out: www.shelemah.com/healthywholesupplylist/

The Must Haves:

Water bottle with ounces marked on it: You want to be able to track how much water you are drinking (2)

Dry brush/Skin brush: Natural bristles and a long handle for reaching your back are important features (5)

Multivitamin: Food based vitamins are best – look for organic and non-GMO if possible (2)

Cod Liver Oil Capsules: Keep them in the refrigerator to prevent a fishy after-taste (2)

Probiotic: Look for one that needs to be refrigerated, is non-GMO, and contains at least 2 billion of each probiotic strain (2)

Detox tea: Look for teas that support liver and kidney function. A couple of my favorites, which are widely available, are *Yogi* brand Peach Detox and *Traditional Medicinal's* Everyday Detox. My favorite loose-leaf is K-Teas System Support, available online www.k-teas.com (4)

Journal: This book has some space to answer questions and keep your logs, but you will probably want more journaling space for devotions (2)

The Helpful to Haves:

Coloring Book: A great mental relaxer and way to stay focused while praying. (2)

Fitbit: Tracks your activity levels for you. The Fitbit One is my favorite model because it tracks steps, flights of stairs, and sleep. (1)

Enzyme Supplements: Even with a good diet, our bodies often lack the enzymes needed to properly digest food and absorb nutrients. Enzyme supplements can be taken with meals to aid in this process (2)

(Note: Make sure any supplements you take are high-quality and food based. *Lab Door* provides great ratings of supplements for purity and effectiveness www.labdoor.com)

Weekly Guides

WEEK 1: NOTICE

"Look among the nations! Observe! Be astonished!

Wonder! Because I am doing something in your days—

You would not believe it if you were told."

Habakkuk 1:5 (NASB)

Welcome to week one! This week you won't be making any changes, but simply observing the lifestyles you already have. You'll be keeping several logs, recording your baselines, expanding your beliefs, and setting your goals. At the beginning of each weekly guide, there is a to-do list followed by further explanation of each new item introduced that week.

This Week:

Reflect on the limits of your beliefs

Set your goals for the next 60 days

Take your baseline measurements
(Will need scale and soft tape measure, see page 73)

Keep daily logs of diet, activity levels, water consumption, sleep, and mood (Logs start on page 75)

Things You Would not Believe:

When you think about your body, your relationships, your emotions, and your relationship with God, what are some things that you would not believe, even if you were told? What if God spoke directly to your heart and said: "You can lose the weight" – or perhaps "Your anxiety *can* lift." Would you believe Him? What about a restored relationship with your mom? Or an exciting life walking in the Spirit – instead of feeling numb in a church pew? While each of us have our own things we just can't believe, there are amazing breakthroughs waiting for us if we will press in.

Spend some time praying and journaling about the things you would not believe if you were told – about your health, your body, your relationships, your job, your emotions, and your spiritual walk. Bring these limits of your beliefs to God and ask Him what He has for you instead. If you aren't sure how to listen for God's voice, check out Appendix 12 (page 67) for some helpful tips.

Dream with God about what the next 60 days could mean for you – body-mind-spirit. And when you do, remember that you are praying "to Him that is able to do far more abundantly beyond all that we could ask or imagine." Ephesians 3:20 (NASB, paraphrased)

Setting Goals:

Now that we have worked on expanding our beliefs, let's start defining what success will look like for this challenge. Write down some of the physical, mental, emotional, spiritual, and lifestyle goals would you like to achieve by the end of this 60 day period.

Keep in mind that goals should be specific, measureable, achievable, realistic, and have a designated time frame. For example, rather than just, "have a better walk with God," be specific, "have a 30 minute devotion time at least 3 days a week." For each goal, you should be able to answer this question: "How will I know if I've achieved this – or at least made progress towards it?"

WEEK 2: SHIFT

"Beloved, I pray that in all respects

you may prosper and be in good health,

just as your soul prospers."

3 John 1:2 (NASB)

Congratulations – you've made it through the first week! This week, we will review the goals you've set and begin to make some shifts in our body and spirit towards a healthy lifestyle. to start this week, I encourage you to read Appendix 2 (page 41) for some tips on building sustainable habits. And don't worry, the logs you keep for the rest of the challenge are not as intense as last week's!

This Week:

Review your logs and goals

Take multivitamin, cod liver oil, and probiotic daily

Drink enough water each day

10 minutes a day in prayer, reading scripture, personal worship time

Review Goals:

Take a few minutes to look over your logs from last week. Do you notice any patterns?

Now look over your goals. Are there any goals you need to adjust based on your logs from last week? If so, what are your new goals?

Supplements:

Use the log on page 91 to help you keep track of your daily supplements. Make sure to eat some food before taking your multivitamin; taking them on an empty stomach can cause an upset stomach. Pick a time of day that you can incorporate taking your supplements into a routine you already follow. For example, taking your supplements every morning right after brushing your teeth. For more information on why I recommend the specific supplements used in this challenge, check out Appendix 3 (page 43).

Hydration:

Staying hydrated is one of the simplest and most important things we can do for our health. But unfortunately, studies show that 75% of Americans are chronically dehydrated.[2] To determine how much water you should drink each day, use the following formula:

(Your weight in lbs.) / 2 = (oz. of water you should drink daily)

On days that you are more active or it is hot outside, you will need to drink more than this minimum to stay hydrated. For more information on how hydration affects our bodies, check out Appendix 4 (page 47).

Devotions:

"Because people are having real, and helpful, spiritual experiences in certain areas of their lives – such as worship, prayer, Bible studies, and fellowship – they mistakenly believe they are doing fine, even if their relational life and interior world is not in order. This apparent 'progress' then provides a spiritual reason for not doing the hard work of maturing."

– Peter Scazzaro in *Emotionally Healthy Spirituality*

Devotions – prayer, Bible reading, worship, etc. – should not something we check off a list and call "done." We do devotions to *change*, not to finish.

Each day this week, set aside 10 minutes to read the Bible and pray. Don't set up an agenda, just set aside the time – offering it to the Lord and inviting Him to do with as He pleases. Then press in to the hard work of letting Him mature you spiritually. As you read, ask yourself the question: "Do I live like this is true?" If not, ask the Lord to help you search your heart and understand why.

Prayer is simply talking with God. As you talk with Him during your devotions be sure to allow time to listen as well. Prayer also has more than just a spiritual effect – spending just 12 minutes a day in focused prayer over a 60-day period can have such an impact that the changes can be seen on a brain scan.[3]

If you have struggled to maintain consistent devotional time in the past – do not be discouraged. Experiment this week with where this 10 minute slot fits most naturally into your everyday life. If you go over 10 minutes that is fine, but don't feel pressure to go any longer than that yet. For more guidance on creating a devotional time, read Appendix 5 (page 49).

WEEK 3: CLEANSE

"Cleanse me with hyssop, and I will be clean;

wash me, and I will be whiter than snow."

Psalm 51:7 (NIV)

This week, we will shift our focus from external habits to inward reflection and cleansing. Often, when we hear "cleanse," we think of a physical cleanse – but this cleanse involves our spiritual and emotional being.

This Week:

10 minutes a day in prayer, reading scripture, personal worship time

Increase daily activity levels

Eat real food

Continue to take multivitamin, cod liver oil, and probiotic daily

Continue to drink enough water each day

Devotions:

During your devotions this week, spend a couple of minutes uncovering the lies in your life. Ask God to help you identify what lies you are believing and then replace them with His truth. Some examples are:

What lies am I believing about my body?

What lies am I believing about finances?

What lies am I believing about You, God?

What lies am I believing about how other people see me?

You can start with those, and of course add your own.

After you ask God to reveal a lie, listen and wait for Him to answer. The reply may come quickly or He may reveal it to you later on through an experience or impression. When you identify a lie, write it down, laugh at it[17], and then ask the Lord what the truth is and listen.

Activity Levels:

This week, look back over your average activity levels from week one and work on increasing those levels. If you walked 2,000 steps a day in week one, find ways to increase your step count until you're hitting 5,000 steps a day or more. Anything below 5,000 steps a day is considered sedentary, and can lead to negative health consequences over time.[4] If you worked out 3 days a week, look for ways to vary the types of exercise or spread them throughout the day. Everyone's activity needs will be different. Rather than setting strict goals, our focus will be on increasing your overall activity level. Be sure to log your activity each week to track your progress from week one. And remember – small increases count! Check out Appendix 7 (page 55) for more information on maintaining an active lifestyle.

Eat Real Food:

This challenge isn't about a particular diet – it's about eating *real food*. Obviously there is more to well-rounded nutrition than just eating *real food*, but it is a great place to start. *Real food* is free from artificial ingredients, minimally processed, and – *ideally* – organic and local. In fact, many of the diseases our culture now considers normal are connected to the Modern American Diet of "food-like substances" rather than real food.[5] When we feed our bodies nutrient-rich, whole, real food, we are setting ourselves up for success instead of failure.

There is a common myth that eating organic real foods costs more than eating the highly processed modern American diet. The truth is you can shop frugally for organic just like you can highly processed. Look for store brand organics just like you would non-organic and try places like Whole Foods and Aldi's, which have a larger selection of store brand organics than most grocery stores. The upfront costs may sometimes be higher, but keep in mind that organic food has a higher nutrient density – which means that your body requires smaller portions of it to be full. Not only will you save money from smaller portion sizes, but the health costs you will avoid by eating real food will save you money in the long run.

Once you have gotten in the routine of eating real food, work on eating nutritionally balanced meals. While a nutritionist or dietitian can help you know the exact nutrient needs for your body, you don't have to be a nutritionist to know what a balanced meal is – or know that you need to eat more vegetables.[5] The USDA "My Plate" guidelines are a great place to start for understanding proper portion size and what each portion should contain.[14] Check out the "Top 10 Food Rules" section in Appendix 6 (page 51) for some great guidelines to eating real food and balanced meals.

WEEK 4: RELEASE

"Whenever you are praying, forgive,

if you have anything against anyone,

so that your Father who is in heaven

will also forgive you your transgressions."

Mark 11:25 (NASB)

This Week:

Add 5 minutes to your daily prayer, reading scripture, personal worship time

Focus on forgiveness in prayer

Drink 1 cup of detox tea daily

Continue to increase daily activity levels

Continue to eat real food

Continue to take multivitamin, cod liver oil, and probiotic daily

Continue to drink enough water each day

Devotions:

This week, increase your devotion time to 15 minutes. From this week on, you will add 5 minutes each week. By the end of the challenge, you will have gone from 10 minutes a day to 40 minutes a day. Even after the challenge ends, keep experimenting until you reach the length of time you can maintain.

You can even try spreading your devotions throughout the day – with 10 minutes in the morning and 20 at night, for example – instead of doing it all at once. See what fits into your rhythm of life. And if you miss a day, don't beat yourself up! We celebrate progress over perfection.

The focus of this week's devotion is *forgiveness*. As this week's verse indicates, forgiveness is something we should practice whenever we pray and it releases us to be forgiven as well.

At the beginning of your devotion time this week, write down the names of people you need to forgive. If no one comes to mind, pray and ask the Lord to reveal if there is someone you are harboring unforgiveness towards. It may even be yourself you need to forgive.

Even if you don't *feel* like forgiving someone, you can make the conscious choice that you *want* to forgive them. A common misconception is that if we forgive someone, we have to rebuild a relationship with them – but that is not true. Forgiving them does not justify their actions or mean that we must feel safe with them in the future. Forgiveness simply means that we are letting go of our need to be the judge and jury over their wrongdoing – and that we trust that the Lord makes a far better judge and jury than we do.

Because forgiveness has to do with resentments we hold in our own hearts, sometimes we need to forgive a person even when they didn't actually do anything wrong. One example is how a child might ask their mom for cookies right before bed, but she says "no." Mom didn't do anything wrong; she was being a good mom. But the child may still need to forgive her for the resentment they hold in their heart. In the same way, we may even need to forgive God for any resentments we've held against Him. For more on forgiveness see Appendix 8 (page 57).

As you go through your list of people you need to forgive you can pray something as simple as this:

I forgive _____ for _____.

(You may need multiple statements for the same person)

When you say a forgiveness statement, it helps to say the statement three times and tap continually on the side of your fingertips. Using the index finger on one hand, tap on your index finger the other hand when forgiving yourself. When forgiving God, tap your middle finger. And when forgiving others, tap your pinky finger. When you are done with the forgiveness statement tap the side of your hand as a way to say, "all done." The tapping and repetition work together with the meridian system of your body to bring your whole being into alignment with your intention to forgive. Read more about the meridian system in Appendix 10 (page 63).

Detox Tea:

Now that you have had a few weeks of eating real food, we will add one cup of detox tea a day for the next two weeks. Detox tea stimulates your body's garbage disposal system and supports your detoxifying organs to get rid of toxins that have been stored.[6] (<u>Note</u>: Check with your doctor if you are pregnant, nursing, or have any conditions that may be affected before using a detox tea.) For more information on detoxing, check out Appendix 9 (page 61).

WEEK 5: RENEW

"If we confess our sins, He is faithful and

righteous to forgive us our sins and

to cleanse us from all unrighteousness."

1John 1:9 (HCSB)

This Week:

Add 5 minutes to your daily prayer, reading scripture, personal worship time

Focus on repentance in prayer

Drink 1 cup of detox tea daily

Dry brush before showering each day

Continue to increase daily activity levels

Continue to eat real food

Continue to take multivitamin, cod liver oil, and probiotic daily

Continue to drink enough water each day

Devotions:

Add another 5 minutes to your devotional time this week. Focus on asking the Lord to reveal places of unrepentance and bitterness in your heart. Last week we forgave others, this week we ask for forgiveness ourselves.

Much of this work will done through prayer and asking the Lord for forgiveness, but there may also be people in your life that you need to reach out to and ask for forgiveness as well. Be open to the Lord's leading this week. Repentance is not intended to be a scary thing. It is designed to keep us close to the Lord and allow us to live in freedom.

Dry Brushing:

Dry brushing helps stimulate your body to release toxins, supporting the detox we began last week with the tea. It provides numerous benefits including increased circulation, better lymphatic function, improved skin condition, and greater mental alertness.[7]

Dry brush every day before you shower, while the water is heating up. Start at your feet and brush your skin towards your heart – and do the same with your arms. On your stomach, brush in a clockwise motion. On your chest and back, brush upwards towards your heart. (Note: Check with your doctor if you have diabetes or circulatory issues before dry brushing.)

WEEK 6: CONNECT

"They were unified as they worshiped together.

In homes, they broke bread and shared meals

with glad and generous hearts.

Acts 2:46 (ESV, author's paraphrase)

This Week:

Add 5 minutes to your daily prayer, reading scripture, personal worship time

In devotional time ask Jesus what He thinks of you

Eat 1 meal a day with someone

Get 8-10hrs of sleep each night

Dry brush before showering each day

Continue to increase daily activity levels

Continue to eat real food

Continue to take multivitamin, cod liver oil, and probiotic daily

Continue to drink enough water each day

Devotions:

Add another 5 minutes to your devotional time this week. This week, focus on asking Jesus what He thinks about you. He may answer you right away or later on in the week through an experience, a dream, or many other ways. Expect that He will answer and be ready to listen. If the answer to what He thinks about you is anything but positive, that's not an answer coming from Jesus – keep listening. See Appendix 12 (page 67) for more on learning to hear God's voice.

Meals:

There is so much power of connection in sharing a meal with someone. One meal each day this week eat with someone and actually connect, put the phones down, and really listen. Maybe it's breakfast with a roommate, dinner with your spouse, or grabbing lunch with a coworker, but each day find one meal that you can share with another person.

Sleep:

Remember when we talked about Americans being chronically dehydrated? Well guess what – we are also chronically sleep deprived.[8] Many of us have settled into a rhythm of getting 6 or less hours of sleep a night, when our bodies need at least 8. Make it a priority this week to get 8-10 hours of sleep each night. Start by figuring out what time you need to get up and then counting back 9 hours – that is the latest you should be getting ready for bed in order to allow 30 minutes for your body to fall asleep.

Bonus challenge: Put your phone away 30 minutes to an hour before you go to bed. No lying in bed, mindlessly scrolling through your Pinterest or Facebook feed. Even with the new night-shift feature on the iPhone, staring at a screen before bed engages our brains in a way that makes it more difficult for us to fall asleep. You might even consider moving your phone charger to the other side of your bedroom so you aren't tempted to grab your phone out of habit. Check out Appendix 11 (page 65) for more information on the importance of sleep and tips on increasing your hours of sleep.

WEEK 7: GIVE SPACE

"He brought me out to a spacious place;

He rescued me because He delighted in me."

Psalm 18:19 (HCSB)

This Week:

Add 5 minutes to your daily prayer, reading scripture, personal worship time

Pray for specific people this week

Create your spacious place

Continue to get 8-10hrs of sleep each night

Continue to dry brush before showering each day

Continue to increase daily activity levels

Continue to eat real food

Continue to take multivitamin, cod liver oil, and probiotic daily

Continue to drink enough water each day

Devotions:

Make a list of no more than 10 people you want to pray for this week. Family members, friends, coworkers, or people you are struggling to love are a great place to start. Spend some time in your devotions praying for each of these people. You may pray for a few of them each day, choose one day to pray for all of them, or pray for all of them every day. If you don't know how to pray for someone else, start by talking to God about the good things you desire for that person. The practice of interceding for others is an important part of a vibrant prayer life. Many intercessors keep a list of those they are praying for, and many even have set days on which they pray for certain people or issues.

Create Your Spacious Place:

Your home is supposed to be your "spacious place" (Psalm 18:19) where you feel revived. But for many of us, our homes end up being a source of stress. When we own more things than we need or can even enjoy – our stuff ends up owning us! Take some time this week to get rid of things you no longer need, use, or find beautiful anymore. Start with one room that you can make your spacious place, and continue to work on the rest of house over the next few weeks.

WEEK 8: REFLECT

"Therefore if anyone is in Christ,

they are a new creature; the old things passed away;

behold, new things have come."

2 Corinthians 5:17 (NASB)

How have you become a new creature through this journey? The promise of old things passing away and new things coming isn't a one-time promise. Every time we enter the presence of the Lord we are inviting Him to strip old things away and let new things come.

This week we're not adding any new practices – stay the course of the continuing the lifestyle habits you have been building.

This Week:

Take your post challenge measurements

Keep logs each day like you did the first week

Add 5 minutes to your daily prayer, reading scripture, personal worship time

Continue to get 8-10hrs of sleep each night

Continue to dry brush before showering each day

Continue to increase daily activity levels

Continue to eat real food

Continue to take multivitamin, cod liver oil, and probiotic daily

Continue to drink enough water each day

Devotions:

Ask God to show you the ways you have already become a new creature throughout this challenge. Talk with Him about what He wants you to have learned from it.

WEEK 9: MAINTAIN

"Because of the mercies of Adonai

we will not be consumed,

for His compassions never fail.

They are new every morning!

Great is Your faithfulness."

Lamentations 3:22-23 (TLV)

You did it! You just devoted eight weeks to pursuing healthy lifestyle changes for your entire body-mind-spirit! This week, reflect back on your journey. Compare the measurements you took before and after the challenge. Look back through your activity logs, taking note of any patterns. Remember, not every change you made will have stuck – but stick with the ones that did! After reflecting this week, you may simply decide to maintain these changes that stuck. Or you might want to go back through the 8-week process again to work on some other changes you want to stick.

This Week:

Maintain the changes that have stuck

Look over your measurements and logs and look for patterns

Thank the Lord for this journey, and ask Him what dreams or journeys He has next for you.

Appendix

How to use the Fitbit App with just Your iPhone

If you have an iPhone 5s or newer you can use it as your tracker and get many of the same benefits as using a Fitbit tracking device.

1. First go to Applications and download the Fitbit app
2. Once it's installed, open the app, and click "Join Fitbit"
3. Then click on "No Fitbit Yet?"
4. Next click on "Set Up Your Fitbit Phone"
5. Now set up an account with Fitbit, click "Let's Go"
6. Enter your height, gender, weight, and age

Your height, weight, gender, and age will all help Fitbit calculate how many calories you burn throughout the day including your basal metabolic rate – the calories that you would burn even if you laid perfectly still all day.

7. Now enter your name, email, and create a password. This makes it super easy to login to your Fitbit account online to view your data or when you switch phones save all your previous data.

That's it! Your phone is now ready to track your daily step count through the Fitbit app. As long as you have your phone on you, it will count your steps throughout the day. You can also manually track your calorie intake, water consumption, exercise and other things.

For some added fun, you can connect your Fitbit app to Facebook and add your friends to compete in challenges against each other!

Appendix 1   How to use the Fitbit App with just Your iPhone

30 Second Habits

Yes, you read that right. 30 second habits. Not minutes, but seconds. Building habits can be difficult. We've all tried at one point to build a new habit – whether it is eating more vegetables, exercising more, or having a daily prayer time. While we may have good intentions and a strong motivation to build these new habits, we have all failed to make lasting changes.

The problem is not our good intentions or the habits we desire to create. The problem is in how we think about building those habits. Trying to make even a 30 minute change is pretty huge in terms of our daily routines. So rather than trying to set aside 30 minutes a day to pray or exercise, we need to think in terms of 30 second habits.

30 second habits refer to small actions that take 30 seconds or less to complete. They are most effective when built into routines we already follow. For example:

Instead of, "I'm going to read for 30 minutes every night before I go to bed." A 30 second habit would be, "After I brush my teeth at night, I will pick up my book." The 30 second habit is simple enough that you can do it every time, regardless of whether you end up reading for your overall goal of 30 minutes.

Habits are best built around a routine you already have a strong instinct to follow, such as brushing your teeth. Over time, other 30 second habits may need to be built up to reach your overall habit goal. First you may focus on picking up the book every night, maybe next you focus on reading the first line of the page.

Even something little like taking a supplement every day will become routine faster if you tie it to routines you already have. So instead of deciding to just take a supplement every day, take your supplements around another routine – like after eating breakfast. Eventually your 30 second habits will build into the lifestyle patterns you wish to have.

As you think of the habits you want to build and the 30 second habits that will get you there it helps to write out your script:

"After I ____; I will _____."

Repeating these scripts to ourselves strengthens the habit and helps build new neural pathways in our brains.[16]

Supplements

Before we talk about what supplements I recommend taking, let's get some things clear: I am a firm believer that we should not *need* to take supplements. If we eat nutritionally dense and balanced meals we should get all the macro and micronutrients our bodies need from our food. Unfortunately, most of us haven't gotten the whole "eating nutritionally dense and balanced meals" thing down very well; and even those of us who do have areas of struggle where we're not getting everything we need.

Another issue is that our food is not as nutrient-rich as it was when our grandparents were our age. Industrial farming practices, GMOs, and the distance our food travels before we eat it all contribute to stripping even the healthiest of foods of their rich nutrients. Growing your own vegetable garden, buying from local farmer's markets, and seeking out organic produce can help increase your nutrient density. However, there still may be gaps in the nutrition your body is getting.

That said, this is why I recommend three primary supplements. You should always check with your doctor about the supplements you are taking to ensure they will not conflict with any medications or medical conditions. But the three I recommend are almost universally agreed to be beneficial.

Multivitamins

Multivitamins are a great foundational supplement to get a wide variety of nutrients. When you pick a multivitamin, look for one that is food based and organic, (or at least non-GMO). Food based vitamins make a big difference, because they are in a form our bodies readily recognize and can absorb. Dr. Axe has a great video explaining this in depth:
https://www.youtube.com/watch?v=ODdx1b27Wmo

Cod Liver Oil (or another omega-3)

Before your gag-reflex kicks in, it's not as gross as it sounds. Cod liver oil comes in capsules as well as straight liquid form, and if you refrigerate the capsules there won't be a fishy aftertaste.

The reason this supplement is important is that it supports brain health, growth, and development. According to some studies, it may even reduce the risk of several diseases including dementia, cancer, cardiovascular disease, and arthritis.[15] Another great resource from Dr. Axe explains the benefits of Omega-3s in more detail:
https://draxe.com/fish-oil-benefits-health/

Probiotics

Researchers are finding more and more that gut health is vitally important for our overall health. A major component of gut health is gut bacteria. Probiotics provide our bodies with the beneficial bacteria strains that help keep our guts happy and healthy. When choosing a probiotic, you want to look for one that needs to be refrigerated and that has a minimum of 2 billion of each probiotic strain it contains.

For these supplements and any others you may take, www.LabDoor.com is a great site for reviewing the quality and efficacy of a supplement to help you choose ones that your body can actually absorb.

Hydration

Anyone who knows me can tell you that I am passionate about hydration. Back in college I heard two statistics in the same week which, put together, were very startling:

1) Americans have the greatest access to clean drinking water

2) 75% of Americans are chronically dehydrated

When I heard these two stats together, it really convicted me that, in a sense, I am dishonoring those who would drink the water if they had access, by not drinking when I do have access.

So while we still need to fund projects like Charity Water and work hard to increase the global access to clean drinking water, we can start by making sure we are staying hydrated. In case you need more convincing, here are some of the ways being chronically dehydrated makes your life suck: fatigue, constipation, skin problems, obesity, and premature aging just to name a few.

So now that you're on board with the whole "we should stay hydrated" idea, here are:

5 Ways to Stay Hydrated

1. Drink Enough Water: I know, duh, right? But to drink enough we need to know how much our bodies need. One way to calculate how many ounces of water you should drink a day is to take your weight in pounds and divide by two. The number you get is how many ounces you should be drinking a day. For example: 130lbs / 2 = 65. So that person should drink about 65 ounces of water a day.

2. Get a Water Bottle: You are much more likely to drink water if you carry it with you. Get a good reusable bottle that has the ounces marked on it and is BPA free. My favorite is a 32oz Nalgene bottle.

3. Set Reminders: Even if you are carrying a Nalgene full of water around all day, it can be easy to forget to actually drink water. I love the app *Gallon a Day*, because it reminds me a few times an hour to drink more water. The free version will give you basic reminders and let you track how much you're drinking.

4. Buddy System: Find a friend who also wants to focus on drinking more water and start a friendly competition. Who can hit their goal the most days in a row?

5. Flavor It: If you can't handle the taste of straight water, try adding some fruit like citrus, strawberries, or cucumber (I know, not a fruit). While there are commercial options out there to flavor your water, sticking with the natural options is usually best to avoid added calories and sugar. You might be thinking, "I drink flavored water every morning... coffee-flavored." The problem with coffee, however, is that it is a diuretic – which means it actually tells your body to dump water, leaving you more dehydrated.

How to Have a Devotion Time

Having a regular devotion time is something Christians have struggled with for decades. I love this excerpt from Elisabeth Elliot because it shows that our struggle to be consistent in devotions is not a new issue in our busy modern era. It was just as much a struggle back in the 1960s as it is now.

> "Having a quiet time with the Lord every day is absolutely essential if you expect to grow spiritually. But you have to plan it. It won't "just happen." We're all much too busy. Early morning is best, and there are plenty of scriptural precedents for that (Jesus rose "a great while before day"; the psalmist said, "In the morning shalt Thou hear my voice").
>
> If you meet the Lord before you meet anybody else, you'll be "pointed in the right direction" for whatever comes. God knows how difficult it is for some to do this, and if you have a reason you can offer Him why early morning won't work, I'm sure He'll help you to find another time. [...] At any rate, plan the time. Make up your mind to stick with it. Make it short to begin with – fifteen minutes or so, perhaps. You'll be surprised at how soon you'll be wanting more."
>
> – Elisabeth Elliot in "*Keep a Quiet Heart*"

While the struggle to keep a regular devotion time is not new, it is not a struggle that has to defeat us. As Elisabeth Elliot says, "It won't 'just happen." You have to be intentional.

Even if you are intentional with the time, the next struggle seems to be what to do during devotional time. The real answer to that question is that there is no real answer. For instance, there is no right answer of how to go on a date with someone you love. But like "dinner and a movie" is a popular dating option, there are popular devotional options as well. Don't feel like you have to follow others' preferred options – do what works for *your* relationship with God. Here are some suggestions to get you started:

Read Scripture: Pick a verse or book of the Bible to meditate on, find a reading plan to follow, or just flip open your Bible and see what the Holy Spirit highlights. As you read, ask yourself what the passages are saying about who God is, who you are, and what Kingdom life looks like.

Pray: Prayer does not have to be a formal well thought out monologue. Prayer is just talking to God and listening to Him. You can pray about things going on in your life, people you have a heart for, questions you have – really anything at all.

Worship: Put on some good worship music or sing some songs yourself. Worship doesn't require a full band or fancy vocals.

Color: Yes, color. Some of my best devotional times have been spent coloring and listening to worship music while I talk to God. Coloring has a way of focusing our thoughts while allowing our minds to wander.

Journal: Many people find journaling to be helpful for focusing during prayer or being able to track answered prayers.

Top 10 Food Rules

Rules taken from Michael Pollan's *Food Rules*
Explanations from Leah Lesesne

1. Eat mostly plants, especially leaves Very few of us have to be told to eat more protein or carbohydrates. But we all tend to struggle with eating enough vegetables. The "My Plate" guidelines from USDA recommend half of every meal to be fruits and vegetables.[14] Dark green leafy vegetables are some of the best for nutrient density.

2. Avoid food products that contain more than 5 ingredients This rule will help you steer clear of most highly processed foods, but there are some exceptions. For example, an organic pasta sauce may have more than 5 ingredients because it lists basil, oregano, thyme, marjoram, and garlic. So, while five is a good number to aim for, the ingredients themselves are more important than the number of ingredients.

3. Shop the peripheries of the supermarket and stay out of the middle Most grocery stores stock their real foods like produce, dairy, meats, and fresh breads along the perimeter of the store; and their processed foods in the middle. By shopping the peripheries, you are more likely to buy nutrient dense real foods.

4. Avoid food products containing ingredients no ordinary human would keep in the pantry Do you keep maltodextrin, high fructose corn syrup, or red dye 40 in your pantry? Then you probably don't want them in the foods you buy either. Steering clear of ingredients your can't pronounce or wouldn't keep in your own pantry will help you avoid a majority of highly processed foods.

5. It's not food if it's called by the same name in every language You can go to any country and order a Coke and a Big Mac without having to speak the local language. Foods that are clean and healthy tend to have their own names in every language. For example, strawberries are called *fraises* in French, *Erdbeeren* in German, and *jordgubbar* in Swedish.

6. Eat animals that have themselves eaten well You are what you eat, and you are also what your meat eats. Animals that are raised on antibiotics and steroids have been fed diets that are meant to fatten them up quickly without regard for what their bodies are designed to eat. When you eat their meat, you are consuming these antibiotics and steroids, as well as any diseases resulting from their improper diet.

7. Eat sweet foods as you find them in nature Cutting sweets out completely can be really difficult. So instead of villainizing all sweets, stick to fruits packed with natural fiber which helps our bodies digest sugars in the healthiest way possible.

8. Eat all the junk food your want as long as you cook/bake it yourself Chances are you are not going to bake cookies, make fried chicken, or crank out some ice cream every day. Eating only the junk food you've made at home gives your total control over the ingredients and naturally limits how often you eat them.

9. Eat when you are hungry, not when you are bored (or stressed, or sad, or angry) We tend to overeat and eat lots of carbohydrate heavy foods when we are bored. Dr. Caroline Leaf also warns against eating when we are stressed, sad, or angry because of *how* our bodies digests the food when we are experiencing those emotions.[5] We actually miss out on nutrients and can make ourselves sick by eating when we are in a negative emotional state.

10. Try not to eat alone When we eat alone, we tend to overeat. Eating with others we tend to eat slower and smaller quantities and we gain not only the nutritional benefits of our meal but the relational and emotional benefits too.

Active over Exercise

When we talk about having an active lifestyle, it's easy to just think about exercise. And while exercise can be an important part of an active lifestyle, it's not the only way to be active.

The Department of Health and Human Services recommends that adults get a minimum of 150 minutes of moderate intensity activity a week.[9] Moderate intensity activities are ones where you can still talk while doing them, but would have difficulty singing. Some examples are brisk walking, gardening, biking, yoga, and Pilates.

If you are not getting anywhere close to 150 minutes of exercise a week right now, don't beat yourself up! Rather than going from 0 to 150 overnight, work on increasing by 10-15 minutes a day until you reach 150 a week. Start with a walk in the mornings or after dinner, try some yoga or Pilates workouts (YouTube has a ton of great free ones), or find ways to simply move more throughout your day.

Setting dedicated exercise time is one way to maintain an active lifestyle, but it's best to incorporate these activities throughout your day. For example: biking to work, walking more, or gardening. A Fitbit can help you track these activity levels throughout your day and see how minor changes – like parking farther away when running errands – can make a big difference in step counts.

How Forgiveness Sets us Free

One of the best parables of forgiveness comes from Matthew 18. Jesus tells the story of the servant who is forgiven much, but then refuses to forgive a lesser debt owed to him. Ultimately the servant is thrown in prison for refusing to forgive.

"So also my heavenly Father will do to every one of you, if you do not forgive your brother from your heart."
Matthew 18:35 (ESV)

Forgiveness is not as much about setting free the person who has wronged you as much as it is about setting *yourself* free. Unforgiveness places you in a self-made prison to which only you hold the key:

"For if you forgive others their trespasses, your heavenly Father will also forgive you, but if you do not forgive others their trespasses, neither will your Father forgive your trespasses."
Matthew 6:14-15 (ESV)

When you refuse to forgive others, you also prevent yourself from receiving forgiveness. Resentments become buried deep in your heart, and over time can become hidden and forgotten… All the while, you remain in your self-made prison.

So how do you recognize unforgiveness, when you've been hurt by someone?

- Do you have strong emotional reactions when you see the person who hurt you?
- Do you want a relationship with the person, or do you try to avoid them?

- Do you rehearse the "speeches" you'd like to deliver?
- Do you imagine ways of getting even or getting revenge?
- Can you sincerely bless this person?
- Do you honestly rejoice when good things happen for the person who has wounded you?

Other signs of unforgiveness may have nothing to do with the person who wounded you:

- Difficulty in relationship with God
- Physical problems
- Difficulty sleeping or resting
- Physical, emotional, mental exhaustion or torment
- Continual patterns of sin or difficulty

These signs may be caused by other factors, but when we experience them it is important to consider if we are harboring any unforgiveness.

Who and what do we need to forgive? Often we think of specific things people have done to wrong us. But sometimes we need to forgive someone for not doing something – like forgiving a parent for not being there when we needed them. We may need to forgive ourselves. It is even possible that we need to forgive God. Even though God is perfect and has done no wrong, we may feel hurt by Him and be holding unforgiveness towards Him.

Forgiveness *does not* mean that we must deny our hurt or anger, or that we have to work to change our feelings. It doesn't mean we have to forget that the offense happened or that what the person did to us was okay. It doesn't mean that the person who hurt us should not be held accountable for their actions. It doesn't mean we have to trust them or restore a relationship with them. Forgiveness is not the same as reconciliation. Reconciliation takes two people and means that the other person is willing to apologize and repair the relationship. Forgiveness only requires you.

Forgiveness *does* mean that we allow God to take away the bitterness and resentment in our hearts and set us free from our self-made prisons. It *does* mean that we give up our right to be the judge and jury over the person who harmed us – trusting that God makes a better judge and jury than we do. It *does* mean that we get to walk in freedom.

Detox All the Things

Detoxes are all the rage in holistic health right now – juices, teas, waters, diets, pills. Everyone is telling you that you need to detox and that you need their product to do it. But here's the truth – your body is already designed to do a fantastic job at detoxing itself!

So is there any value to the detox fad? Yes – but it's not the products themselves that do the detoxing, *and* you don't need some expensive detox program. Your body does the detoxing, and the products just support your body in what it already knows how to do.

The first and most important step in detoxing is to stop putting toxins in your body. Just a few weeks of drinking plenty of filtered water and eating only organic and non-GMO allows your body to naturally detox itself of many pesticides and chemicals. In fact, eating strictly organic for just a week eliminates about 90% of the pesticide load in your body.[10]

After giving your body a break from toxins, drinking a detox tea and dry brushing encourages your liver and kidneys to keep functioning at peak performance. Without an official detox, your body would continue detoxing all on its own, but many people have seen great results from doing a detox program to support their body's work.

Meridian Lines and Tapping

Meridian lines are the system of pathways in the body by which energy flows. Energy meaning: electrical, physical, scientific energy – not "mystical" energy as some in the New Age movement describe it. It is the system that acupuncturists, chiropractors, and energy psychology practitioners use to alleviate physical and emotional symptoms.

Unlike chakras, meridian lines have a growing body of scientific evidence to back up what Eastern medicine has known for centuries – that they are real. Researchers have shown, through energetically-charged photo luminescent material injected at acupuncture points, that there is a flow to energy in the human body.[12] And the wavelike patterns of that flow follows the meridian line charts used in acupuncture and chiropractic work.[12] Other research has found physical evidence of a previously unrecognized primo vascular system which follows the meridian line charts as well.[13]

The way acupuncture works with meridian lines is by placing pins as little antennas to draw the flow of energy around any blockages in the meridian lines. Chiropractic uses physical manipulations to put the body back into alignment wherever the improper flow in the meridian lines has pushed the body out of alignment.

The problem acupuncturists and chiropractors both have run into, however, is that their adjustments do not always stick. The meridian lines have not been dealt with directly, just the physical symptoms of the meridian lines being blocked have been dealt with. This is where energy psychology methods such as N.E.T., EFT, and Splankna have made huge strides in dealing with the emotional blockages – complimenting the work of chiropractic and acupuncture.

When we experience trauma, our bodies store an energetic signature of the emotions we feel within the meridian system. When these blockages are not dealt with, we continue to have the same symptoms over and over. Thus, we need the same chiropractic adjustments over and over or feel stuck in our emotional responses.

Splankna is the very first Christian protocol for dealing with the emotional blockages in the meridian system. Through a combination of intention and circuitry, we clear the emotional blocks and allow breakthrough where there were once barriers.

One tool from Splankna is tapping your fingers while you say a forgiveness statement. The tapping of fingers engages the circuitry of the meridian system, and the forgiveness statement sets your intention to forgive.

A similar tapping tool that can be used in many ways is a collarbone statement. By repeating a truth statement three times while tapping continually on your collarbones, you help your whole body-mind-spirit to come into alignment with the truth. Scriptures are great truth statements to try this with.

More information about the Splankna Therapy model and its approach to energy psychology from a Christian perspective can be found at their website, www.splankna.com

Sleep

Remember when you were a kid and your mom would tell you to go to bed, and you thought sleep was the worst thing in the world? As adults, we seem to have the same aversion to going to bed – all the while wishing we could get more sleep.

Americans are chronically sleep deprived, and with that comes a host of health problems.[8] A weakened immune system, memory problems, depression, heart disease, and weight gain are all issues that can be related to sleep deprivation.[11]

Knowing you need more sleep is easy, but actually getting that sleep is the hard part. Start with giving yourself enough time for 8-10 hours of sleep each night. This takes some discipline, and requires knowing what time you need to wake up the next morning. Once you have created adequate time for sleep, work on creating a positive sleep environment. Remove distractions like phones and TVs, close curtains to get the room as dark as possible, and keep the temperature cooler.

Many people's struggle with sleep is not the time required, but the actual act of falling asleep. Having a higher activity level during the day, avoiding caffeine and alcohol (especially close to bedtime), and drinking enough water can all help. Herbal remedies such as valerian root and chamomile can help as well, but check with your doctor or naturopath before using any kind of sleep aid – herbal or not. (Note: Do not take chamomile while pregnant, as it has been shown to cause miscarriage)[18]

Hearing God's Voice

Training your "ears" to hear God's voice begins with learning to discern the voices you listen to on a daily basis. There are four voices you may be hearing at any given time: God's voice, the enemy's voice, your voice, or other people's voices. Each voice is distinct and there are some characteristics you can listen for to help discern whose voice it is.

God's voice: Always loving. May convict, but does not condemn – speaks life, hope, and redemption. Always agrees with Scripture, just maybe not our wounded understanding of Scripture.

The enemy's voice: Steals, kills, and destroys. Full of shame, death and condemnation – sounds accusatory and creates negative thoughts about yourself. Uses "you" language instead of "I", and often feels intrusive. Contradicts, twists, or half-truths Scripture.

Your voice: Feels familiar. May be positive or negative, but the lines of thought are traceable. Uses "I" or "me" language.

Other people's voices: May be positive or negative. You tend to be able to remember who said it and when it was said.

When trying to discern a voice, think about how the voice and its words make you feel. Do you feel loved and accepted? Or do you feel shameful, like you need to hide? How the voices we listen to make us feel says a lot about who is speaking.

Ways to Grow in Hearing:

The best way to grow in hearing is to listen. Start asking God questions, especially silly little ones you could easily test for the answer. Questions like "What color will the next car that drives past me be?" Or asking Him to tell you the name of your server at a restaurant. There are plenty of little questions like this that you can use to test out your hearing.

God's voice can come to you in many ways. You may not hear an audible voice, but you might have thoughts that don't quite feel like your own thoughts. Other ways He speaks are through the Bible, dreams, visions, everyday experiences, and other people. Trust that He knows how to speak to you in a way that you can hear. The Holy Spirit is your guide to hearing God's voice and will teach you how you listen.

For more on learning to hear God's voice, check out *Hearing 101* by Faith Blatchford.

Weekly Logs

Get the Healthy & Whole app to track your measurements and logs on your phone. Available in the Apple app store November 1st 2016

BASELINES

Take these baseline measurements on day 1 so you can look back on them at the end of the challenge.

Height (in):

Weight (lbs.):

Hip (in):

Waist (in):

Bust (in):

Thigh (in):

Upper Arm (in):

Any Current Health Problems:

Average Daily Mood (Put an X on the line):

Terrible---Fantastic

Average Feeling of Closeness to God (Put an X on the line):

Super Far---Super Close

WEEK 1 LOGS

Fill this log out each day for the first week of the challenge.

A Fitbit activity tracker can be helpful for tracking steps/active minutes and sleep, and the Fitbit app can also be used to track water intake and food. The Fitbit app can be used even without a Fitbit; download the app and in settings choose add device. It will give you the option to use your phone as the tracking device. For step-by-step instructions for setting up the Fitbit app to work with just your phone see Appendix 1 on page 39.

DAY 1

Water (oz.)	
Food (What was it and how much? Calories or portion size)	Breakfast: Lunch: Dinner: Snacks:
Sleep (hours and quality)	

Step count/active minutes	

Average Mood (Put an X on the line):

Terrible---Fantastic

Average Feeling of Closeness to God (Put an X on the line):

Super Far---Super Close

Time Spent in Prayer/Devotions	

DAY 2

Water (oz.)	
Food (What was it and how much?)	Breakfast: Lunch: Dinner: Snacks:
Sleep (hours and quality)	

Step count/active minutes	

Average Mood (Put an X on the line):

Terrible--Fantastic

Average Feeling of Closeness to God (Put an X on the line):

Super Far--Super Close

Time Spent in Prayer/Devotions	

DAY 3

Water (oz.)	
Food (What was it and how much?)	Breakfast: Lunch: Dinner: Snacks:
Sleep (hours and quality)	

Step count/active minutes	

Average Mood (Put an X on the line):

Terrible--Fantastic

Average Feeling of Closeness to God (Put an X on the line):

Super Far---Super Close

Time Spent in Prayer/Devotions	

DAY 4

Water (oz.)	
Food (What was it and how much?)	Breakfast: Lunch: Dinner: Snacks:
Sleep (hours and quality)	

Step count/active minutes	

Average Mood (Put an X on the line):

Terrible--Fantastic

Average Feeling of Closeness to God (Put an X on the line):

Super Far---Super Close

Time Spent in Prayer/Devotions	

DAY 5

Water (oz.)	
Food (What was it and how much?)	Breakfast: Lunch: Dinner: Snacks:
Sleep (hours and quality)	

Step count/active minutes	

Average Mood (Put an X on the line):

Terrible--Fantastic

Average Feeling of Closeness to God (Put an X on the line):

Super Far---Super Close

Time Spent in Prayer/Devotions	

DAY 6

Water (oz.)	
Food (What was it and how much?)	Breakfast: Lunch: Dinner: Snacks:
Sleep (hours and quality)	

Step count/active minutes	

Average Mood (Put an X on the line):

Terrible---Fantastic

Average Feeling of Closeness to God (Put an X on the line):

Super Far--Super Close

Time Spent in Prayer/Devotions	

DAY 7

Water (oz.)	
Food (What was it and how much?)	Breakfast: Lunch: Dinner: Snacks:
Sleep (hours and quality)	

Step count/active minutes	

Average Mood (Put an X on the line):

Terrible---Fantastic

Average Feeling of Closeness to God (Put an X on the line):

Super Far--Super Close

Time Spent in Prayer/Devotions	

WEEK 2 LOGS

Supplement	Day 1	Day 2	Day 3	Day 4	Day 5	Day 6	Day 7
Multi-Vitamin							
Cod Liver Oil							
Probiotic							

	Day 1	Day 2	Day 3	Day 4	Day 5	Day 6	Day 7
Use this space to tally bottles* of water drank							

*1 bottle = _____ oz.

	Day 1	Day 2	Day 3	Day 4	Day 5	Day 6	Day 7
Devotion Time							

WEEK 3 LOGS

Supplement	Day 1	Day 2	Day 3	Day 4	Day 5	Day 6	Day 7
Multi-Vitamin							
Cod Liver Oil							
Probiotic							

	Day 1	Day 2	Day 3	Day 4	Day 5	Day 6	Day 7
Use this space to tally bottles* of water drank							

*1 bottle = _____ oz.

	Day 1	Day 2	Day 3	Day 4	Day 5	Day 6	Day 7
Activity							

	Day 1	Day 2	Day 3	Day 4	Day 5	Day 6	Day 7
Devotion Time							

WEEK 4 LOGS

Supplement	Day 1	Day 2	Day 3	Day 4	Day 5	Day 6	Day 7
Multi-Vitamin							
Cod Liver Oil							
Probiotic							

	Day 1	Day 2	Day 3	Day 4	Day 5	Day 6	Day 7
Use this space to tally bottles* of water drank							

*1 bottle = _____ oz.

	Day 1	Day 2	Day 3	Day 4	Day 5	Day 6	Day 7
Activity							

	Day 1	Day 2	Day 3	Day 4	Day 5	Day 6	Day 7
Detox Tea							
Devotion Time							

WEEK 5 LOGS

Supplement	Day 1	Day 2	Day 3	Day 4	Day 5	Day 6	Day 7
Multi-Vitamin							
Cod Liver Oil							
Probiotic							

	Day 1	Day 2	Day 3	Day 4	Day 5	Day 6	Day 7
Use this space to tally bottles* of water drank							

*1 bottle = _____ oz.

	Day 1	Day 2	Day 3	Day 4	Day 5	Day 6	Day 7
Activity							

	Day 1	Day 2	Day 3	Day 4	Day 5	Day 6	Day 7
Detox Tea & Dry Brushing							

	Day 1	Day 2	Day 3	Day 4	Day 5	Day 6	Day 7
Devotion Time							

WEEK 6 LOGS

Supplement	Day 1	Day 2	Day 3	Day 4	Day 5	Day 6	Day 7
Multi-Vitamin							
Cod Liver Oil							
Probiotic							

	Day 1	Day 2	Day 3	Day 4	Day 5	Day 6	Day 7
Tally bottles* of water drank							

*1 bottle = _____ oz.

	Day 1	Day 2	Day 3	Day 4	Day 5	Day 6	Day 7
Activity							

	Day 1	Day 2	Day 3	Day 4	Day 5	Day 6	Day 7
Hours of Sleep							

	Day 1	Day 2	Day 3	Day 4	Day 5	Day 6	Day 7
Devotion Time							

	Day 1	Day 2	Day 3	Day 4	Day 5	Day 6	Day 7
Dry Brushing							

WEEK 7 LOGS

Supplement	Day 1	Day 2	Day 3	Day 4	Day 5	Day 6	Day 7
Multi-Vitamin							
Cod Liver Oil							
Probiotic							

	Day 1	Day 2	Day 3	Day 4	Day 5	Day 6	Day 7
Tally bottles* of water drank							

*1 bottle = _____ oz.

	Day 1	Day 2	Day 3	Day 4	Day 5	Day 6	Day 7
Activity							

	Day 1	Day 2	Day 3	Day 4	Day 5	Day 6	Day 7
Hours of Sleep							

	Day 1	Day 2	Day 3	Day 4	Day 5	Day 6	Day 7
Devotion Time							

	Day 1	Day 2	Day 3	Day 4	Day 5	Day 6	Day 7
Dry Brushing							

POST CHALLENGE MEASUREMENTS

Take these post challenge measurements to compare to your baseline measurements from week 1

Height (in):

Weight (lbs.):

Hip (in):

Waist (in):

Bust (in):

Thigh (in):

Upper Arm (in):

Any Current Health Problems:

Average Daily Mood (Put an X on the line):

Terrible--Fantastic

Average Feeling of Closeness to God (Put an X on the line):

Super Far--Super Close

WEEK 8 LOGS

Fill this log out each day for the eighth week of the challenge.

DAY 1

Water (oz.)	
Food (What was it and how much?)	Breakfast: Lunch: Dinner: Snacks:

Sleep (hours and quality)	
Step count/active minutes	

Average Mood (Put an X on the line):

Terrible---Fantastic

Average Feeling of Closeness to God (Put an X on the line):

Super Far---Super Close

Time Spent in Prayer/Devotions	

DAY 2

Water (oz.)	
Food (What was it and how much?)	Breakfast: Lunch: Dinner: Snacks:
Sleep (hours and quality)	

Step count/active minutes	

Average Mood (Put an X on the line):

Terrible---Fantastic

Average Feeling of Closeness to God (Put an X on the line):

Super Far---Super Close

Time Spent in Prayer/Devotions	

DAY 3

Water (oz.)	
Food (What was it and how much?)	Breakfast: Lunch: Dinner: Snacks:
Sleep (hours and quality)	

Step count/active minutes	

Average Mood (Put an X on the line):

Terrible--Fantastic

Average Feeling of Closeness to God (Put an X on the line):

Super Far--Super Close

Time Spent in Prayer/Devotions	

DAY 4

Water (oz.)	
Food (What was it and how much?)	Breakfast: Lunch: Dinner: Snacks:
Sleep (hours and quality)	

Step count/active minutes	

Average Mood (Put an X on the line):

Terrible--Fantastic

Average Feeling of Closeness to God (Put an X on the line):

Super Far---Super Close

Time Spent in Prayer/Devotions	

DAY 5

Water (oz.)	
Food (What was it and how much?)	Breakfast: Lunch: Dinner: Snacks:
Sleep (hours and quality)	

Step count/active minutes	

Average Mood (Put an X on the line):

Terrible--Fantastic

Average Feeling of Closeness to God (Put an X on the line):

Super Far---Super Close

Time Spent in Prayer/Devotions	

DAY 6

Water (oz.)	
Food (What was it and how much?)	Breakfast: Lunch: Dinner: Snacks:
Sleep (hours and quality)	

Step count/active minutes	

Average Mood (Put an X on the line):

Terrible---Fantastic

Average Feeling of Closeness to God (Put an X on the line):

Super Far--Super Close

Time Spent in Prayer/Devotions	

DAY 7

Water (oz.)	
Food (What was it and how much?)	Breakfast: Lunch: Dinner: Snacks:
Sleep (hours and quality)	

Step count/active minutes	

Average Mood (Put an X on the line):

Terrible--Fantastic

Average Feeling of Closeness to God (Put an X on the line):

Super Far--Super Close

Time Spent in Prayer/Devotions	

REFERENCES

1. http://www.huffingtonpost.com/james-clear/forming-new-habits_b_5104807.html

Lally, P., van Jaarsveld, C. H. M., Potts, H. W. W. and Wardle, J. (2010), How are habits formed: Modelling habit formation in the real world. Eur. J. Soc. Psychol., 40: 998–1009. doi:10.1002/ejsp.674

2. http://www.medicaldaily.com/75-americans-may-suffer-chronic-dehydration-according-doctors-247393

3. How God Changes Your Brain: Breakthrough Findings from a Leading Neuroscientist– March 23, 2010 by Andrew Newberg M.D, Mark Robert Waldman. P26,27.

http://drleaf.com/blog/how-prayer-affects-the-brain/

4. http://well.blogs.nytimes.com/2016/04/01/ask-well-does-less-than-5000-steps-a-day-make-you-sedentary/?_r=0

 Tudor-Locke, C. & Bassett, D.R. How Many Steps/Day Are Enough? Preliminary Pedometer Indices for Public Health (2004) Sports Med 34: 1. doi:10.2165/00007256-200434010-00001

5. Leaf, Caroline (2016), Think and Eat Yourself Smart

6. Cline, John C, MD, BSc, IFMCP. Close:block:scholUnivAuthors Open:block:publicationBlock Alternative Therapies in Health and Medicine Close:block:publicationBlock 21.3 (May/Jun 2015): 54-62.

7. http://articles.mercola.com/sites/articles/archive/2014/02/24/dry-skin-brushing.aspx

8. http://www.cdc.gov/features/dssleep/

9. https://health.gov/paguidelines/guidelines/chapter1.aspx

10. Oates, Liza, Marc Cohen, Lesley Braun, Adrian Schembri, and Rilka Taskova. "Reduction in Urinary Organophosphate Pesticide Metabolites in Adults after a Week-long Organic Diet." *Environmental Research* 132 (2014): 105-11. Web.

11. http://www.healthline.com/health/sleep-deprivation/effects-on-body

12. http://www.ncbi.nlm.nih.gov/pmc/articles/PMC3838801/

13. http://www.ncbi.nlm.nih.gov/pmc/articles/PMC3793287/#B2 http://www.jams-kpi.com/article/S2005-2901(13)00208-2/fulltext

14. https://www.choosemyplate.gov/dietary-guidelines

15. https://draxe.com/fish-oil-benefits-health/

16. *Leaf, Caroline (2007), Switch on Your Brain*

17. https://www.youtube.com/watch?v=tNxurOKCAy8

18. Bhaskaran N, Shukla S, Srivastava JK, Gupta S. *Chamomile: an anti-inflammatory agent inhibits inducible nitric oxide synthase expression by blocking RelA/p65 activity.* Int J Mol Med. 2010 Dec; 26(6):935-40.

Sridharan S, Archer N, Manning N. *Premature constriction of the fetal ductus arteriosus following the maternal consumption of chamomile herbal tea.* Ultrasound Obstet Gynecol. 2009 Sep; 34(3):358-9.

RECOMMENDED RESOURCES

Books:
Splankna by Sarah Thiessen
Switch on Your Brain by Dr. Caroline Leaf
Think & Eat Yourself Smart by Dr. Caroline Leaf
Keep Your Love On by Danny Silk
Culture of Honor by Danny Silk
Sozo by Dawna DeSilva and Theresa Liebscher
The Maker's Diet by Jordan Rubin
Healthy & Free by Beni Johnson
Becoming Myself by Stasi Eldredge
Emotionally Healthy Spirituality by Peter Scazzaro
Hinds Feet on High Places by Hannah Hurnard
The Seven Mountain Prophecy by Johnny Enlow
Healing the Orphan Spirit by Leif Hetland
The 30 Day Faith Detox by Laura Harris Smith
Hearing 101 by Faith Blatchford
Food Rules by Michael Pollan
Keep a Quiet Heart by Elisabeth Elliot
What Happens when Women Pray by Evelyn Christenson
You're Crazy if You Don't Talk to Yourself by Steve Backlund
Let's Just Laugh at That by Steve Backlund
Living from the Unseen by Wendy Backlund
The Veil by Blake Healy
Orthodoxy by G.K. Chesterton
The Biblical Guide to Alternative Medicine by Dr. Neil T. Anderson and Dr. Michael Jacobson

Websites:
Splankna Therapy Institute www.splankna.com
Bethel Sozo ministry www.bethelsozo.com
Elijah House Prayer Ministry www.elijahhouse.org
16 Personalities www.16personalities.com
Lab Door www.labdoor.com

Apps:
Healthy & Whole
Gallon a Day
Fitbit
Bible.is
Happify
Recovery Record (*advertised for eating disorders but great for tracking food and moods in general*)

Music:
Housefires www.housefires.org
IHOP Prayer Room Live Stream www.ihopkc.org/prayerroom/
United Pursuit www.unitedpursuit.com
Bread & Wine www.breadandwineonline.com
Healing Frequencies www.healingfrequenciesmusic.com

Misc:
Edens Garden Essential Oils www.edensgarden.com
K-Teas www.k-teas.com

About the Author:

Leah Lesesne *(pronounced lay-uh like the princess and luh-sane)* lives in downtown Atlanta with her husband Tommy and their urban farm full of critters. She holds a masters in professional counseling, is a graduate of Elijah House School of Prayer Ministry, and is a certified Splankna practitioner. After working for a few years as a counselor, she stepped away from the mental health field to pursue her first loves of inner healing prayer ministry and holistic health.

For more information about her work:

Website www.Shelemah.com

Instagram @ShelemahCoaching

Facebook www.facebook.com/ShelemahCoaching

Made in the USA
Charleston, SC
22 November 2016